TIME CAPSULE:
THE BOOK OF RECORD

TIME CAPSULE:

THE BOOK OF RECORD

THOMAS B. ALLEN

ROGER MACBRIDE ALLEN

Time Capsule: The Book of Record

ISBN: 0-9818487-6-1
ISBN-13 978-0-9818487-6-1

The Westinghouse Electric and Manufacturing Company registered the copyright of the original text and design of *The Book of Record* in 1938. The copyright of *The Book of Record* was not renewed, and the work is in the public domain.

All text in the present volume, aside from the facsimile pages (pages 23 to 78) copyright © 2010 Thomas B. Allen and Roger MacBride Allen.

FoxAcre Press
Takoma Park, Maryland
www.FoxAcre.com
TimeCapsuleBook.com

TABLE OF CONTENTS

Acknowledgements

We would like to acknowledge the kind assistance of Mr. David Grinnell, Chief Archivist at the Library and Archives Division of the Sen. John Heinz History Center, Pittsburgh, Pennsylvania, who led us through the Archive's materials related to the Westinghouse exhibits at the World's Fairs.

We are likewise indebted to Ms. Catherine Keen, Associate Curator of the Archives Center of the National Museum of American History, who provided access to the Edward J. Orth Memorial Archives of the World's Fair, 1939-1940.

Both of them made real and generous efforts to allow us access to papers and collections related to the Time Capsule and *The Book of Record*. Our thanks to each of these most helpful scholars, and to the institutions they represent.

TBA
RMA

THE TIME CAPSULE AND
THE BOOK OF RECORD:
AN INTRODUCTION

BY

THOMAS B. ALLEN & ROGER MACBRIDE ALLEN

IT IS A STARTLING NOTION to most people that someone had to *invent* the Time Capsule. The idea is, these days, so obvious, so universal, so well-understood by everyone, that it seems strange to think that it was not always there. More startling still, then, to learn that it was invented as recently as 1938.

There had been cornerstones laid long before that time, and people had tucked artifacts in them, or locked items away in safes with the idea that someone would look at them in the future. However, the concept of a purpose-built object filled with artifacts and information about the present, sealed up with the sole intention of delivering its contents to a future time, did not exist until G. Edward Pendray dreamed it up because his boss asked for a promotional idea connected to the NewYork World's Fair of 1939.

Pendray thought big, and decided to send his creation five thousand years into the future. But how, he wondered, could he be sure that anyone in the year 6939 would learn about his Time Capsule? His answer, as we shall see, was *The Book of Record,* a facsimile of which you now hold in your hands.

If the Time Capsule is the buried treasure, *The Book of Record* is the treasure map. (It does in fact include a map—with a dot instead of an X to mark the spot; see page 68.) But maps and books wear out, or are destroyed, or are lost. By printing thousands of copies, Pendray made it more likely that at least one book would survive. Pendray foresaw that *The Book of Record* would need to be reprinted from time to time, in order to improve the odds that word would get through to 6939. In fact, it is entirely possible that the copy you are now reading will be the one found, studied, and copied in 2110 AD, thus passing the word to 2210, and 3010, and on into the future, a vital link in the chain between our recent past and our remote future.

No other time capsule project has included anything like *The Book of Record*. But to tell the story of *The Book of Record* properly, we must first tell the tale of The Time Capsule itself.

FIVE THOUSAND YEARS
FROM YESTERDAY

ON SEPTEMBER 23, 1938, a distinguished group of men, many in top hats, solemnly gathered on soggy land that once had been a dump in the Borough of Queens. At precisely the moment of the Autumnal Equinox, and to the toll of a large gong borrowed from Chinatown, a torpedo-shaped metal capsule was lowered into a fifty-foot shaft.

This was the ceremonial burial of The Time Capsule into "The Well of the Future" (which was renamed "The Immortal Well" by the time the Fair opened) on the site of what would become the 1939-1940 New York World's Fair. The Time Capsule was the world's first deliberately manufactured archaeological artifact: Its only purpose was to be found by the people of the future. It was the first true Time Capsule, the inspiration for the thousands of time capsules that have since been buried, entombed, and walled-up all over the world.

The capsule was "the message of present-day America to the people of Earth of 6939 A.D." Coiled in rolls of microfilm were ten million words—from *True Confessions Magazine* to the *Encyclopedia Britannica* and the lyrics of "Flat Foot Floogee." And packed in the capsule were hundreds of objects, including a can opener and a fountain pen, a safety pin and a rhinestone clip, golf balls, a lady's hat from a famous designer, and a Mickey Mouse watch.

The people who buried the Time Capsule believed—or at least hoped—that "Futurians" of 6929 would seek out the Time Capsule. But who would those Futurians be? What sort of world would they live in?

The theme of the 1939 World's Fair was "The World of Tomorrow," with the clear implication that such a World would be a better place than the world of the 1930s. But when the people who created the Fair and the Time Capsule looked ahead, they saw not one, but two futures.

One was a smooth and streamlined world full of technological wonders, ideal cities, high-speed steamships, bullet-shaped locomotives, and gleaming highways. Visitors to the General Motors Futurama exhibit were given pins that read "I Have Seen the Future," and many believed they had. New inventions, faster and more powerful machines and vehicles, new ways of doing things, new ways of thinking and living would sweep away all the dreary remnants of the Great Depression that still remained. Technology and progress would give the world, especially America, a fresh start, and all would be made bright, clean, rational, streamlined, efficient, peaceful and orderly.

But the other world of tomorrow, seen half-consciously perhaps, was a shattered wreck of a globe, done in by the brutal dictatorships so plainly on the march, destroyed by wars more terrible and universal than the Great War that had ended only two decades before. Two years earlier, the 1936 film *Things To Come* had predicted a general war that would start with a sneak attack air raid on Christmas Eve, 1940. That imagined war would go on for decades, reducing all the combatant nations to beggary, with the survivors left to scrabble among the ruins of cities and machines they no longer understood, fighting still, but for reasons they no longer remembered. To anyone who had seen the battlefields of the Great War, that future seemed entirely believable.

And so, the Time Capsule was designed to be recovered not only by people using advanced excavation techniques but also by people who had forgotten virtually all the technologies that had gone into building the capsule; people who had lost virtually all records of the English language; people who lived in a world that would not know where New York had been, or how to build a metal detector. Some of the contents of the Time Capsule are plainly expected to be perceived as quaintly amusing to advanced Futurians, while others almost seem to be included as a way to re-introduce science and technology that the collapsed Futurian civilization will have forgotten.

TO HELP THE FUTURIANS of whatever kind recover the Time Capsule, its creators distributed a guidebook to libraries, museums, convents, and lamaseries throughout the world. The guide, entitled *The Book of Record of the Time Capsule of Cupaloy*, gave the navigational coordinates of Flushing Meadows in Queens and told Futurians how to find the buried capsule (in a section titled "Seeking Metallic Substances Beneath the Ground"). As an aid to understanding the narration of newsreels tucked into the capsule, it includes an essay on the presumably lost English language, accompanied by a diagram showing "exactly where each of the 33 sounds of 1938 English is formed in the oral cavity."

The author of that section of the book was Dr. John Peabody Harrington, an eccentric gatherer of vanishing American Indian languages. In 1915 the Bureau of American Ethnology hired him as a research ethnologist, and for nearly forty years he wandered the West, gathering—but rarely publishing—discoveries about more than 125 Indian languages. One of his specialties was the mapping and description of languages no longer spoken.

He assembled an enormous collection of notes about vocabularies, photographs, maps, botanical specimens, and recordings (many on wax cylinders). But much of his work remained unknown because he wanted to keep colleagues from seeing what he had found. He hid material in warehouses, garages, attics, cellars, and abandoned buildings, mostly along the West Coast. Intentionally or not, he left behind his very own collection of time capsules, material he preserved for the future but kept hidden from his competitors. Not until his death in 1961 did Smithsonian Institution curators discover the caches of data. His papers in the archives of the Smithsonian encompass 683 linear feet. Ethnologists of the 21st Century are still deciphering and digitizing about one million pages of his scribbled writing, much of it in code, in Spanish or in a phonetic system that he had developed.

Based on his expertise about dead and dying languages, Harrington predicted that in five thousand years all the languages of 1939 would have "become extinct or so altered as to require a key for their understanding." He provided that key by developing the mouth map for producing English, a thousand-word vocabulary, a phonetically-spelled version of the language ("birds" is written as *bjrdz*, "person" as *pjrsjn*) and sketches for teaching the grammar of English. A sketch of a man with a bow and arrow bears the caption *Rining hic ecmd* (Running he aimed) to demonstrate the idea of one verb being subordinate to another. A sketch to illustrate the tenses—*paest*, *prezjnt* and *fyuctyur*—shows a smoke-puffing steamship traveling from one port to another. Maybe the Futurians would understand the tenses. But would they recognize a steamship, or get the idea that a picture showing travel over water was supposed to illustrate the passage of time?

The Book of Record's grandiloquent, pseudo-biblical language came from the typewriter of G. Edward Pendray, who coined the term "Time Capsule" after realizing that his first choice, "Time Bomb," had a regrettable connotation. Pendray, a pioneering public relations man, had been hired by Westinghouse to improve its stodgy image. Pendray's first brainstorm, the Time Capsule, was "a kind of religious experience for me," he said. He worked out the basics quickly, and then launched into the hurried and often zany process of selecting the Capsule's contents and signing up its contributors, including Albert Einstein. It took about ninety days of frenzied activity to put together the Time Capsule, which was meant to last five thousand years.

As *The Book of Record* describes the Time Capsule's contents, they were chosen to give Futurians "information touching upon all the principal categories of our thought, activity, and accomplishment; sparing nothing, neither our wisdom nor our foolishness, our supreme achievements nor our recognized weaknesses." Whatever Futurians may think of the Time Capsule's contents, the objects, along with the reasons for choosing them, give us a perfectly preserved slice of American social history in the 1930s.

Pendray wrote science fiction and was a founder of the American Rocket Society, predecessor of the present-day American Institute of Aeronautics and Astronautics. One of the first organizations of science fiction writers called itself The Futurians, a name used by many other science fiction groups to this day. In 1931, when Pendray went to Germany to talk with writer Willy Ley about rockets, he met a schoolboy named Wernher Von Braun. During World War II, Von Braun developed rocket weapons for Nazi Germany and, after the war, was a leader of the U.S. space program.

Although Pendray is credited with creating the Time Capsule, he was not the first person to have that kind of brainstorm. In August 1937, Dr. Thornwell Jacobs, president of Oglethorpe University in Atlanta, began working on his plan to create a "Crypt of Civilization." After a complicated series of calculations, Jacobs came to the conclusion that civilization had begun in exactly 4241 B.C.—6,177 years in the past from the time he did his figuring. He decided to set up a cache of materials to be opened in 8113 A.D., exactly 6,177 years in the future, when the mid-twentieth century would be the "midpoint" of civilization.

Thirty-three months later, an astounding amount of knowledge was placed in the Crypt. Workers microfilmed some eight hundred works, including two hundred books of fiction. Also included were drawings of inventions, and records of phenomena from sports and other pastimes to artificial arms and dentures. Items placed in the Crypt included vegetable and fruit seeds, clothing, a glass whiskey jigger, plastic and papier-mâché models of various objects, and a package containing miniature articles of everyday clothing. The collection was placed in what had been a swimming pool in a university building. A massive steel door, the only entrance to the Crypt, was welded shut on May 25, 1940. Photographs of the Crypt interior show an orderly jumble of artifacts that bears a certain resemblance to the pictures of the contents of Tutankhamun's tomb shortly after it was opened in 1922.

There was a vague sense of competition between the two projects at the time, but thanks to the publicity that Pendray generated, the Westinghouse Time Capsule almost entirely eclipsed the Crypt of Civilization. A message to the Futurians from Jacobs is in the Time Capsule. Somewhat ironically, in 1990, on the fiftieth anniversary of the sealing of the Crypt, Oglethorpe University became the headquarters of the International Time Capsule Society.

THE TIME CAPSULE WAS BURIED at a crossroads in time, when America and the world were nearing the end of peace and the birth of atomic energy. In *The Book of Record* is a letter by Albert Einstein, written in German and translated. "Our time is rich in inventive minds, the inventions of which could facilitate our lives considerably," he wrote. ". . . We have learned to fly and we are able to send messages and news without any difficulty over the entire world through electric waves. However, the production and distribution of commodities is entirely unorganized so that everybody must live in fear of being eliminated from the economic cycle, in this way suffering for the want of everything. Furthermore, people living in different countries kill each other at irregular time intervals, so that also for this reason any one who thinks about the future must live in fear and terror...."

A year later, Einstein would send another letter. That one, to President Roosevelt. would launch America's atomic bomb project. A copy of that letter would be placed in Time Capsule II, buried at the end of the 1964-1965 New York World's Fair.

The precise moment of the Autumnal Equinox of 1938 was not

selected as the moment to bury the capsule because it actually had any meaning; it was pulled out of thin air by Pendray because it seemed scientific and solemn, and because it matched up with the Fair's construction schedule. However, the date and the event signified more than the planners had ever intended. In Europe, the Munich crisis was approaching its climax. Within a week of the Time Capsule's burial, no thinking person could seriously believe that war could be far off or that the United States could remain uninvolved. The illusion of isolationism as a practical policy was starting to fade. More than the Time Capsule was buried that day. So too was the false innocence of America that inspired its attempts to stand aloof from foreign entanglements. It was the exact moment when all the old certainties and beliefs of the prewar world came into question.

Everyone expected that nearly everything was about to change, and they were right—but most of the results would be nothing like the Fair's wonderful "World of Tomorrow." The Time Capsule, intended as a report on the history of our times to the people of the future, omits all reference to the largest event in recorded history: World War II. So much was changed by the war that ended with Einstein's bomb that there were some suggestions that the Time Capsule be dug up, updated, and reburied. In a sense, that was done when the identically-shaped Time Capsule II was buried alongside its predecessor during the 1964-1965 World's Fair.

The original Time Capsule was born of the tradition of placing objects in the cornerstones of new buildings to be entombed forever as part of the dead past. But the Time Capsule looked forward, not back. It was—and is—about the future. The Time Capsule resembles the streamlined vehicles so celebrated in the 1930s. The Time Capsule was a vehicle designed to travel through time, not space. It was a Time Machine intended to transport us to the Future—or at least to transport the idea of us, as we were at the moment of the Autumnal Equinox of 1938.

All the days of all our lives since, and all days of the rest of your life, and all the days of your children and grandchildren, and their grandchildren, the Time Capsules will be there in Flushing Meadow, not merely waiting, slumbering, but traveling, sailing through the uncertain years to a time that is as unknown to us as it was to the people of 1938, to a time when the Futurians might, if all goes well, greet the arrival of a slender messenger from yesterday's World of Tomorrow.

THE CREATORS of the Time Capsule saw themselves as chroniclers of their era. They looked back five thousand years while looking forward five thousand years. They hoped "that we might leave records of our own day for five thousand years hence; to a day when the peoples of the world will think of us standing at history's midpoint." As contributors to future history, they gave to the world of 6939 A.D their view of the world of 1939. They chose the year 6939 as the year the capsule would be opened because they believed that Futurians would be interested in 1939 A.D. as much as the people of 1939 (and thereabouts) were interested in artifacts from the dawn of recorded history, 5,000 years before 1939. The creators of the Time Capsule (and the Crypt of Civilization) were plainly inspired, at least in part, by the fabulous discoveries being dug out of the Egyptian desert in the 1920s and 1930s.

Five thousand years ago, hunter-gatherers in North America were chipping flints to make projectile points, and in the Middle East craftsmen were working in copper and writing systems were emerging. We know all this from fifth-millennium artifacts that modern archaeologists have dug up. Presumably, archaeologists of 6939 will have a whole treasure chest of artifacts to study when they dig up the Time Capsule.

The Story of the Time Capsule, published by Westinghouse, says that corporation engineers began working on the project early in 1938. They decided that the Capsule would be seven feet, six inches long and eight and three-eighths inches in diameter. It was made of Cupaloy, a copper alloy invented by Westinghouse. *The Book of Record* notes the alloy—99.4% copper, 0.5% chromium, and 0.1% silver—was supposed to resist corrosion because in "electrolytic reactions with ferrous metals in the soil, it becomes the anode and therefore will receive deposits, rather than suffer corrosion." That explanation will likely be no less cryptic in 6939 than it is in our time, but it sounds technical and impressive.

Westinghouse compared Cupaloy to an alloy "reputed to have been used by the ancient Egyptians, the secret of which has been lost." The Capsule consisted of seven cast segments that were threaded, screwed together, and sealed with molten asphalt.

The Capsule's contents were placed in "an inner crypt" lined with Pyrex, an extremely durable type of glass that had been developed by Corning Glass Works in 1915 for use in ovenware. The crypt was embedded in a water-repellent, petroleum-based wax. Air was sucked out of the inner crypt and filled with nitrogen, which was expected to act as a preservative. Many 21st-cenury scientists wonder if this preservative procedure can possibly keep most of the contents from turning to dust.

Pendray was so taken with the design of the Capsule, and with Cupaloy, that he toyed with the idea of promoting miniature Time Capsules, made of Cupaloy and of a size that could be tucked into caskets. These personal time capsules would go in alongside the body of the deceased and could contain whatever documents the deceased (or the loved ones of the deceased) might wish to be found in the distant future. As was the case with Cupaloy itself, the idea didn't catch on.

The *Book of Record*, which would presumably lead Futurians to the Time Capsule, was an integral part of the project. Pendray's fascination with ancient Egypt shows forth in one sentence that warns against premature opening of the Time Capsule. A hint of a mummy's curse lingers in the words: "When it has been brought up out of the ground, let the finders beware, lest in their eagerness they spoil their contents by ill-considered moves." The next sentences are calmer: "Let the Capsule be transported with the utmost care, at once, to a warm, dry place. Cleanse the outside of mud, slime, or corrosion."

Westinghouse's official history of the project, *The Story of The Time Capsule*, says that *The Book of Record* "was prepared after detailed consultation with libraries, museum authorities, printers and bookbinders. Suggestions for binding and general treatment were obtained from the office of the National Archives, the New York Public Library, the American Library Association and other sources." From the U. S. Bureau of Standards came specifications for enduring, 100-pound rag paper. The book was designed and typeset by Frederic W. Goudy, using type that he himself created.

The Story of the Time Capsule asserts that 3,650 copies were printed: 2,000 (including one buried in the Time Capsule) bound in handmade flexible paper and stamped with aluminum; and 1,650 bound in royal-blue buckram stamped with gold. But the scant records about distribution of the *Book of Record* indicate that not all copies found their way, as claimed, to "libraries, museums, monasteries, convents, lamaseries, temples, and other safe repositories throughout the world."

In May 1939, *The New Yorker* reported its results after querying thirty-two intended repositories for *The Book of Record*. Responses raised doubts about the potential 5,000-year life of *The Book of Record*. The librarian of Queen's University in Kingston, Ontario, for example, said that when the book arrived, "I had no illusion as to our ability to preserve it for 5,000 years..." The National Museum of Archaeology in Mexico said the book would be "preserved for as long as the destructive insects, the political eventualities of Mexico, and the carefulness of the librarians will permit." The chief curator of the Belgian Royal Library said that the idea seemed "somewhat infantile." But he placed it on a shelf and vowed that "it will stay there as long as the collections of the

Royal Library last; will that be five thousand years or a few months? Nobody knows. The skies today are full of hostile planes. And nobody can tell what tomorrow will bring." On one of the tomorrows a year later, in May 1940, Germany invaded Belgium.

Concerns about a tomorrow of war haunted the Fair, whose theme was an optimistic preview of the World of Tomorrow. *The Book of Record* contained two grim messages besides the one from Einstein. Robert Andrews Millikan, who, like Einstein, had won the Nobel Prize in physics, leavened his words with hope: "At this moment, August 22, 1938, the principles of representative ballot government, such as are represented by the governments of the Anglo-Saxon, French, and Scandinavian countries, are in deadly conflict with the principles of despotism.... If the rational, scientific, progressive principles win out in this struggle there is a possibility of a warless, golden age ahead for mankind. If the reactionary principles of despotism triumph now and in the future, the future history of mankind will repeat the sad story of war and oppression as in the past."

More metaphysical was the message of Thomas Mann, the German writer who was also a Nobel laureate. He had fled to Switzerland when the Nazis came to power in 1933. "We know now that the idea of the future as a 'better world' was a fallacy of the doctrine of progress," he wrote, undermining the Fair's tub-thumping for progress. "That optimistic conception of the future," he wrote, "is a projection into time of an endeavor which does not belong to the temporal world, the endeavor on the part of man to approximate to his idea of himself, the humanization of man...."

Just short of twelve months after the Time Capsule was buried, about the time the World's Fair was ending the first of its planned two years of operation, World War II erupted, and threatened to sweep away all endeavors of any kind. But the Time Capsule had scarcely begun its journey. It still had 4,999 years to travel.

The Physical Book

Printing and Publishing Details

THE ORIGINAL VERSION of *The Book of Record* was published in 1938 in hard-cover and soft-cover editions. As we have seen, Westingthouse reported that 1,650 copies of the hard-cover book were distributed to libraries and other institutions worldwide. That number is almost certainly inflated, and might actually reflect the number of copies printed, or the number delivered to Westinghouse.

A 1938 list of intended consignees computed a "grand total" of 909 recipients, though not all of these were to receive the hardcover edition. In 1965 a Westinghouse employee researched the point. He interviewed Pendray and wrote in a memo that "only about a thousand ... went to legitimate depositories." Distribution of the soft-covered edition, "bound in handmade flexible paper, stamped with aluminum," was not well documented. These copies were mainly used as promotional materials, and distributed in a fairly casual way. One memo instructs Westinghouse employees to search through the seating area after an event where the books were handed out. They were to collect for reuse any copies that had been left behind.

A copy of the soft-cover version was placed in the Time Capsule itself, as well as in the replica Time Capsule. (It is visible through the cut-away glass panel of the replica.)

Most of the copies printed were in paperback. However, for whatever reason, nearly all of the copies known to the authors are hardcover. The paperback version is the real collector's item.

In the run-up to the 1964-1965 fair, Westinghouse executives and Pendray discovered that G. Leonard Gold, owner of the Prestige Book Company, the printer of The Book of Record, was nearly destitute. After a flurry of memos, they arranged to pay $500 cash for fifty copies of the book, at least in part simply as a way to put money in Gold's hands.

IN 1965, a second Time Capsule was placed in the ground ten feet north of the first capsule. An "addendum" to The Book of Record was distributed in connection with Time Capsule II. An October 1965 Westinghouse memo reports that plans were to send the supplement to "739 depositories." This addendum consisted of nothing more than a slip of paper that could be placed in the front of the original book. It had a "peel and stick" strip to make it easy to glue it in place. Obviously, many recipients of The Book of Record never got this addendum. It is included in this facsimile.

Another insert, confirming that the book was "an authentic copy of The Book of Record," was apparently included in at least some copies of The Book of Record when it was distributed in 1938-1939. This insert page with its statement of authenticity does not appear in all copies of The Book of Record. It was likely not intended to be permanently inserted into the book, but merely included as part of the package shipped to the recipients. Its main purpose appears not to have been to authenticate the book, but rather to encourage the recipient to make sure that the enclosed copy of the book was placed in a permanent location. Its absence, in and of itself, from a particular copy of The Book of Record should in no way cast doubts on the genuineness of that copy.

The hard-cover copies of the original edition of The Book of Record were designed to last as long as possible. They were printed on special cream-colored Permanent Ivory Wove paper, and the pages were laid out with extremely wide margins that will make it easier to rebind worn copies repeatedly as the centuries pass by. The original book pages were approximately 6 $^3/_8$ by 9 $^{15}/_{16}$ inches, and the bound book itself approximately 6 $^5/_8$ by 10 inches.

Although the margins have been adjusted in this edition, the type and illustrations are reproduced in the same size as in the original edition.

The original hard-cover book was published with five entirely blank pages (in other words, two blank sheets plus an additional blank right-hand page) at the front of the book. These totally blank sheets have not been reproduced in this edition.

The original edition of *The Book of Record* was printed in black ink, except for three elements. The following items were colored a shade of red approximating C10 M100 Y70 K0 in the CMYK color printing system:

• The words **THE TIME CAPSULE** on the title page (page 27).

• The large and ornate initial W on the first page of the main text (page 31 in this volume, paginated as page 5 in the original book pages).

• The dot indicating the location of the Westinghouse Time Capsule on the map on page 68 of the present volume. (The map page is un-numbered in the orignal. It faces page 43 in the original page numbering.)

Due to printing and production requirements, the three elements described above are reproduced in greyscale in the present volume.

THE BOOK OF RECORD
OF THE TIME CAPSULE
OF CUPALOY

Blue-buckram hardcover copy of
The Book of Record of The Time Capsule

This is an authentic copy of

THE BOOK OF RECORD OF

THE

TIME CAPSULE

✣

The edition is limited, and it is not expected that the book will ever be reprinted in its present permanent form. It is a message to the future, and should be carefully preserved. If you do not wish to keep it, please send it to a library, museum or other permanent repository.

WESTINGHOUSE ELECTRIC &
MANUFACTURING COMPANY

Note: This statement of authenticity is included in this facsimile edition for purposes of completeness, and its appearance here should not be construed as a claim that the present volume is from the original edition of
THE BOOK OF RECORD.

DEPOSIT OF TIME CAPSULE II

ON OCTOBER 16, 1965, at the close of the New York World's Fair of 1964-1965, Time Capsule II was deposited by the Westinghouse Electric Corporation exactly 10 feet north of the precise location of the original 1938 Time Capsule. That location is LATITUDE 40° 44' 34" .089 north of the Equator, LONGITUDE 73° 50' 43" .842 west of Greenwich.

Time Capsule II preserves for the peoples of 6939 A. D. a record of the vast changes which occurred in the 25-year period following deposit of Time Capsule I.

Time Capsule II contains 117,000 pages of microfilmed information, metal recordings to preserve the voices and music of our time, excerpts of television and motion-picture productions, and objects that are evidence of scientific and technological advances or that represent commonplace things in daily use originated in the past quarter century.

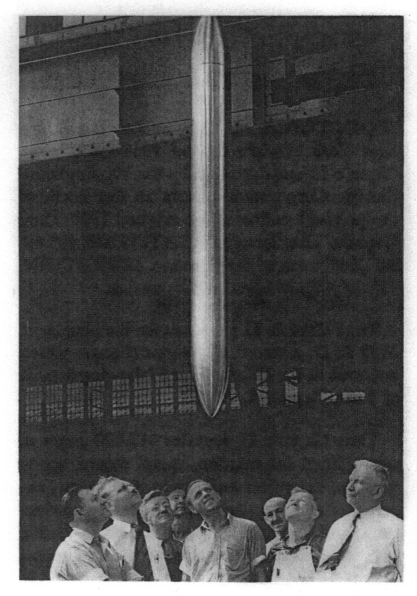

THE ENVELOPE FOR A MESSAGE TO THE FUTURE
BEGINS ITS EPIC JOURNEY

THE BOOK OF RECORD OF
THE
TIME CAPSULE
OF CUPALOY

DEEMED CAPABLE OF RESISTING
THE EFFECTS OF TIME FOR FIVE
THOUSAND YEARS ، PRESERVING
AN ACCOUNT OF UNIVERSAL
ACHIEVEMENTS ، EMBEDDED IN
THE GROUNDS OF THE

NEW YORK WORLD'S FAIR
1939

*All the days of my appointed time will I wait,
till my change come.*

Thou shalt call, and I will answer thee.

—JOB XIV : 14-15.

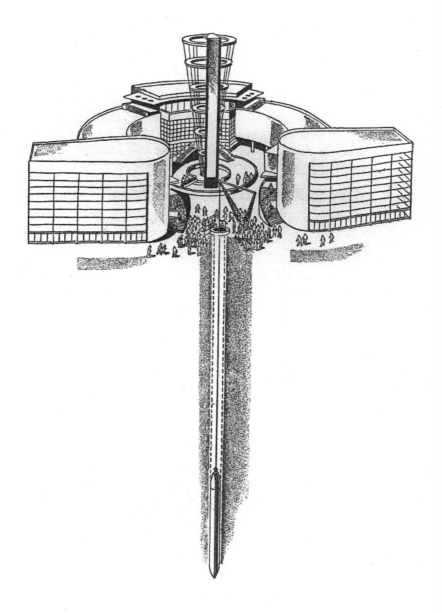

THE TIME CAPSULE

A Segment of Our Time Preserved
for Future Generations

HEN WE SURVEY THE PAST and note how perishable are all human things, we are moved to attempt the preservation of some of the world's present material & intellectual symbols, that knowledge of them may not disappear from the earth.

For there is no way to read the future of the world: peoples, nations, and cultures move onward into inscrutable time. In our day it is difficult to conceive of a future less happy, less civilized than our own. Yet history teaches us that every culture passes through definite cycles of development, climax, and decay. And so, we must recognize, ultimately may ours.

By the same reasoning, there will rise again a civilization of even vaster promise standing upon our shoulders, as we have stood upon the shoulders of ancient Sumer, Egypt, Greece, and Rome. The learned among that culture of the future may study with pleasure and profit things now in existence which are unique to our time, growing out of our circumstances, needs, and desires.

Five thousand years ago, during a period of invention, development, and science rivaling that of our day, recorded history began. It would be pleasant to believe

[5]

that we might leave records of our own day for five thousand years hence; to a day when the peoples of the world will think of us standing at history's midpoint.

Whether we shall be able to transmit such a segment of our time into the future depends not only on our ingenuity at selection and preservation, on the excellence of engineering, metallurgy, chemistry, and other intellectual disciplines, but also in large measure on those who come after us, and their willingness to cooperate in such an archæological venture across the reaches of time.

We pray you therefore, whoever reads this book, to cherish and preserve it through the ages, and translate it from time to time into new languages that may arise after us, in order that knowledge of the Time Capsule of Cupaloy may be handed down to those for whom it is intended. We likewise ask: let the Time Capsule rest in the earth until its time shall come; let none dig it up for curiosity or for any other reason. It is a message from one age to another, and none should touch it in the years that lie between.

PREPARATION OF THE CAPSULE

HOW long the Time Capsule will remain in the earth, or what experiences await it, we have no way of knowing. But if, as is our hope, it rests untroubled until the year A.D. 6939, there may be people capable of discovering and raising it, of reading and studying the contents.

We imagine they will be able to reconstruct, through archæological techniques like those developed in our own time, the hard structures of our culture: our architecture, our dams and roads, our houses, and our general physical appearance, as indicated by our skeletons. But certainly many of the perishable things of our culture will have been lost in the course of time, unless special efforts are made to preserve them.

In these matters we have taken counsel of archæologists, historians, metallurgists, engineers, chemists, geophysicists, and other technical men of our time. We have given much study not only to the selection of the items to be preserved, but also to methods of preserving them for so long a time & of leaving this message about them.

Our first concern was the construction of the Time Capsule itself, a problem of great complexity. Our experience with artificial materials is too short to give us certain knowledge of their ability to withstand the corrosive effects of thousands of years, yet the older mineral materials, including stone and glass, are too brittle and too difficult to work, are liable to breakage from pressure or earthquake, and are too difficult to detect when buried in the earth.

We have decided that the best possible material is a metallic alloy of high corrosion resistance & considerable hardness, of nonferrous nature, and preferably containing a high percentage of copper. Of all the tools used by ancient peoples, those of stone and copper have come down to us from farthest in the past.

It happens that a copper alloy fulfilling these specifications has recently been developed. Known as Cupaloy, it is 99.4 per cent copper, .5 per cent chromium, and .1 per cent silver. This material may be tempered to a hardness similar to that of mild steel, yet has a resistance to corrosion equal to pure copper. In electrolytic reactions

[7]

with ferrous metals in the soil, it becomes the anode and therefore will receive deposits, rather than suffer corrosion, should such action take place. It is our belief that a properly constructed capsule of Cupaloy will withstand the naturally destructive forces of five thousand years, and by its strength protect the contents from the accidents of time.

The Time Capsule is seven feet, six inches in length, and eight and three-eighths inches in diameter. Its Cupaloy shell consists of seven cast segments, all segments except the last solidly screwed together, sealed with molten asphalt, and burnished. The last section, closed after the placing of the contents in the Capsule, is shrunk-fitted on tapering threads.

The inner crypt of the Capsule is a space six & a half inches in diameter & approximately six feet, nine inches in length. Within it is a Pyrex glass envelope embedded in a petroleum base wax. The objects to be preserved are enclosed in the glass, from which all air has been exhausted. The spaces left between the objects in the crypt have been filled with an inert gas, nitrogen, the inactive element which makes up four-fifths of our atmosphere.

The materials inside the crypt have been selected for permanence and have been treated, so far as possible, to give them resistance to time. Material which would ordinarily be published in books has been photographed on acetate microfilm ; a method that not only promises permanence but also makes possible the concentration of much information in small space. Where paper was necessarily enclosed, we have used only the finest 100 per cent rag, fulfilling the specifications of the United

[8]

States Bureau of Standards for permanence. Metal parts which might be subject to attack by moisture have been coated with a thin layer of wax. No acids or corrosive substances are included in the crypt's contents or in the materials with which the Time Capsule is sealed, nor are any materials included which are known to decay or dissociate into corrosive liquids or vapors.

The Time Capsule is die-stamped with this message :

TIME CAPSULE OF CUPALOY, DEPOSITED ON THE SITE OF THE NEW YORK WORLD'S FAIR ON SEPTEMBER 23,1938, BY THE WESTINGHOUSE ELECTRIC & MANUFACTURING COMPANY. IF ANYONE SHOULD COME UPON THIS CAP-SULE BEFORE THE YEAR A. D. 6939 LET HIM NOT WAN-TONLY DISTURB IT, FOR TO DO SO WOULD BE TO DEPRIVE THE PEOPLE OF THAT ERA OF THE LEGACY HERE LEFT THEM. CHERISH IT THEREFORE IN A SAFE PLACE.

The Time Capsule was deposited fifty feet deep in the earth on the site of the building of the Westinghouse Company, on the grounds of the New York World's Fair 1939, by A. W. Robertson, chairman of the Board of Directors of the Westinghouse Electric & Manufactur-ing Company, at 12 o'clock noon, September 23, 1938, the exact moment of the autumnal equinox of that year.

RECOVERY OF THE CAPSULE

WHEN the time has come to dig for the Time Capsule, look for it in the area known as the Flushing Meadows, Borough of Queens, New York City, on the site of the New York World's Fair 1939.

[9]

The appointed year will be, according to our common way of reckoning time, the 6,939th year since the birth of Christ. According to the Jewish calendar it will be the year 10699; according to the Chinese, the 36th year of the 160th cycle; according to the Mohammedan, the 6,469th year since the birth of the Prophet; according to the Buddist, the 7,502d year since the birth of Buddha; according to the Shinto [Japanese], the 7,599th year since the birth of the first emperor, Jimmu Tenno.

If none of these ways of reckoning the years has survived, it still may be recognized by calculation from astronomical data. In the year 1939 there will be two eclipses of the moon, falling respectively on May 3d and October 28th. There will be two eclipses of the sun—an annular eclipse on April 19th, the path of annular eclipse grazing the North Pole of the earth, and a total eclipse on October 12th, the total path crossing near the South Pole.

The heliocentric longitudes of the planets on January 1st at zero-hours Greenwich [midnight] were

Mercury	175°	55′	42″
Venus	124°	43′	32″
Earth	99°	40′	29″
Mars	192°	4′	2″
Jupiter	339°	12′	22″
Saturn	17°	30′	45″
Uranus	46°	23′	31″
Neptune	171°	32′	3″
Pluto	120°	17′	

The mean position of the North Star [Polaris or Alpha Ursæ Minoris] on January 1st will be Right Ascension, 1 hr. 41 min. 59 sec.; North Polar distance, 1° 1′ 33″.8.

[10]

In the opinion of our astronomers, such a combination of astronomical events is unlikely to recur for many thousands of years. By computing backward from their time, people of the future will therefore be able to determine the number of years that have elapsed since our time.

The Capsule lies buried at exactly the point where the centerline of the Westinghouse plot intersects the centerline of the great halls of the Westinghouse World's Fair building. By A.D. 6939, it is probable, all present-day landmarks, city surveys, and other such aids for locating such an object will have disappeared. The spot may still be discovered, however, by determination of the latitude and longitude. The exact geodetic coordinates [North American Datum of 1927] are:

Latitude   40°   44′   34″.089 north of the Equator
Longitude   73°   50′   43″.842 west of Greenwich

These coordinates, surveyed by the United States Coast and Geodetic Survey and given to the thousandth part of a second of arc, are accurate enough to locate an object one-tenth of a foot or less in diameter at a particular position on the surface of the earth.*

It may be that due to shifts of the earth's poles, differences in method, or other causes, this calculation will still not give the exact spot. It may also happen that the Time Capsule will sink or migrate from the point of deposit during the ages. Seekers may nevertheless still find it by the methods of electrical prospecting such as are used in our day for the location of minerals, water, buried metallic objects, and deposits of salt and oil.

*See page 43.

[11]

If electrical instruments similar to those of our time are used to locate the Capsule, it should be indicated by the distortion of a magnetic field, the increased conductivity of the soil, or other such indications. Certain steps have been taken to increase the Time Capsule's responsiveness in this respect. The soil in which the Time Capsule is buried is fairly homogeneous, and though there are scraps of metals, mostly ferrous, buried in it, these should all have disappeared by corrosion before many centuries have passed. On account of the softness of the soil, however, the Capsule may have settled to a greater depth. This possibility should be taken into account.*

When the Capsule at length has been located, a problem will still remain, for if the land is swampy & wet, as in our day, adequate methods must be devised to recover it. The Capsule may be raised by sinking a caisson of such a type as to hold back the mud and water during excavation. Should this prove inexpedient, it may be possible to freeze the soil by cold brine circulating in pipes driven into the earth around the site. When the soil is frozen it may then be dug in the same manner as hard earth.

The Capsule is provided with an eye to which lifting apparatus may be attached. It is likely, however, that this ring may have disappeared through erosion. In this case, the Capsule should be raised gently with a sling.

When it has been brought up out of the ground, let the finders beware, lest in their eagerness they spoil the contents by ill-considered moves. Let the Capsule be transported with the utmost care, at once, to a warm, dry place. Cleanse the outside of mud, slime, or corrosion.

*See page 39.

[12]

Then cut off the top carefully at the deeply scored groove which has been left to guide the saw.

Should gas rush out when the inner glass is punctured, or when the saw penetrates the crypt, let there be no alarm, for this is a harmless gas enclosed as a preservative.

THE CONTENTS OF THE CAPSULE

WITHIN the limitations imposed by space, the problems of preservation, and the difficulty of choosing the truly significant to represent all the enormous variety and vigor of our life, we have sought to deposit in the Time Capsule materials and information touching upon all the principal categories of our thought, activity, and accomplishment; sparing nothing, neither our wisdom nor our foolishness, our supreme achievements nor our recognized weaknesses.

We have included books and pictures that show where and how we live: some in apartments like dwellers in cliffs, but comfortably; others in detached houses; still others moving about the country in homes mounted on wheels.

We have set forth the story of our architecture, by which we have reared soaring pinnacles into the sky.

We have described the offices and the factories where we work, the machines that write, compute, tabulate, reproduce manuscript a thousandfold, sort out, and file; the machines that stamp and fashion metals; the machines and methods with which metals are knit together by electricity and cut apart by gas; the complex techniques of mass production, with which articles that consist of scores of different materials, requiring hundreds of operations to assemble, can nevertheless be sold among us for a few cents.

We have described in text and picture the arts and entertainment of our day; the games we play; the history & development & present attainments of painting, sculpture, music, the theater, motion pictures, and radio.

We have included copies of representative newspapers & magazines of this day, containing news, articles, fiction, and advertisements broadly characteristic of our period. We have also included a novel, the most widely read of our time. For good measure we have added specimens of our cartoons and "comics," such as daily and weekly delight millions in our newspapers and in our moving picture theaters.

Ours is a day of many faiths. We have provided descriptions of the world's religions, numbered their followers, and enclosed the Holy Bible, a book which is the basis of the Christian faith. We have provided outlines of the world's principal philosophies. We have discussed the all-pervading and effective educational systems of our time, and told in text and pictures the story of the training of our young.

We have included a copy of our Constitution, and something about our government, under which we live as free men, ruled by our own elected representatives chosen at regular intervals by the votes of all, both men and women. We have included, also, a history of our country and a chronological history of the world.

Our scientists have measured the speed of light and compared the distances of the planets, stars, and nebulæ; they have charted the slow evolution of primal proto-

[14]

plasm into man, fathomed the ultimate composition of matter and its relation to energy, transmuted the elements, measured the earth and explored it, harnessed earthquake, electricity, and magnetism to probe what lies beneath our feet; they have shifted the atoms in their lattices and created dyes, materials, stuffs that Nature herself forgot to make. The stories of these achievements have been set forth in the Time Capsule.

Our engineers & inventors have harnessed the forces of the earth and skies and the mysteries of nature to make our lives pleasant, swift, safe, and fascinating beyond any previous age. We fly faster, higher, and farther than the birds. On steel rails we rush safely, behind giant horses of metal and fire. Ships large as palaces thrum across our seas. Our roads are alive with self-propelling conveyances so complex the most powerful prince could not have owned one a generation ago; yet in our day there is hardly a man so poor he cannot afford this form of personal mobility.

Over wires pour cataracts of invisible electric power, tamed and harnessed to light our homes, cook our food, cool and clean our air, operate the machines of our homes & factories, lighten the burdens of our daily labor, reach out and capture the voices and music of the air, & work a major part of all the complex magic of our day.

We have made metals our slaves, and learned to change their characteristics to our needs. We speak to one another along a network of wires and radiations that enmesh the globe, and hear one another thousands of miles away as clearly as though the distance were only a few feet. We have learned to arrest the processes of decay; our

[15]

foods are preserved in metal or frost and by these means
we may have vegetables and fruits in any season, delica-
cies from foreign lands, and adequate diet anywhere.

All these things, and the secrets of them, and something about the men of genius of our time and earlier
days who helped bring them about, will be found in the
Time Capsule.

How our physicians have healed the sick, controlled
pain, and conquered many diseases, has been recounted
there; how we have suppressed epidemics through the
enormous undertakings of our system of public health;
how our drugs and biologicals are compounded, and the
enormous and varied list of them.

There are included samples and specimens of the new
materials of our time, created in the laboratories of our
engineers and chemists, on the looms of our mills, and in
the forges, furnaces, and vats of our factories.

There are also samples of the products of our farms,
where machinery has turned scarcity into abundance;
where research has produced plants never seen in nature; where science now is able to produce plants even
without soil.

There are also many small articles that we wear or
use; that contribute to the pleasure, comfort, safety, con-
venience, or healthfulness of our lives; articles with which
we write, play, groom ourselves, correct our vision, re-
move our beards, illuminate our homes and work-places,
tell time, make pictures, calculate sums, exchange values,
protect property, train our children, prepare our food.

Believing, as have the people of each age, that our women are the most beautiful, most intelligent, and best

[16]

groomed of all the ages, we have enclosed in the Time Capsule specimens of modern cosmetics, and one of the singular clothing creations of our time, a woman's hat.

That the pronunciation of our English tongue may not be lost, a "Key to English" has been prepared and printed in this book. That our vocabulary may not be forgotten, we have included in the Capsule a dictionary, defining more than 140,000 common words and phrases. That our idiom may be preserved, we have provided also a dictionary of slang and colloquial expressions. Finally, that our method of writing may be recovered, should all other record of it disappear, we have included a book in which the Lord's Prayer is translated into three hundred different tongues; also the fable "The Story of the North Wind & the Sun" translated into twenty-five languages. These may serve, as did the trilingual Rosetta stone, to help in the translation of our words.

In the Capsule there are only two actual books of our time, in the size and form to which we are accustomed. These are this book and the Holy Bible. All the rest have been photographed page by page on microfilm, which by the small space it requires has permitted us to include on four small reels the contents or equivalent of more than seventy ordinary books—enough in their usual form to fill the Capsule's crypt several times over. A magnifying instrument is included, with which the microfilm may be read.

Should those who recover the Capsule wish to know our appearance, and how we dress, act, and talk, there have been provided two reels of significant and typical scenes of our time, in pictures that move and speak, imprisoned on ribbons of cellulose coated with silver. If knowledge of machines for projecting these pictures and voices has disappeared, the machines may nevertheless be recreated, after recovery of the Capsule, from photographs and descriptions.

Each age considers itself the pinnacle & final triumph above all eras that have gone before. In our time many believe that the human race has reached the ultimate in material and social development; others, that humanity shall march onward to achievements splendid beyond the imagination of this day, to new worlds of human wealth, power, life, and happiness. We choose, with the latter, to believe that men will solve the problems of the world, that the human race will triumph over its limitations and its adversities, that the future will be glorious.

TO THE PEOPLE OF THAT FUTURE
WE LEAVE THIS LEGACY

A KEY TO THE ENGLISH LANGUAGE

Dr. John P. Harrington

ETHNOLOGIST, BUREAU OF ETHNOLOGY
SMITHSONIAN INSTITUTION
WASHINGTON, D C.

Our years are like the shadows
That o'er the meadows fall,
Are like the fragile wildflower
That withers by the wall—
A dream, a song, a story,
By others quickly told,
An unremaining glory
Of years that soon get old.

AFTER five thousand years all the spoken languages of the present time will have become extinct or so altered as to require a key for their understanding. The English language spoken in the United States today, if not replaced by some other natural or invented tongue, will have suffered complete reforming many times over through the laws of linguistic evolving—laws which though proceeding in regular paths will, because of their complexity, work the apparent result of radical havoc. Books of the present day, through chemical change, will have disappeared.

Records of the Etruscan language of ancient Italy in Greek letters which are easily readable have amply survived to the present time, but no one has been able to understand the words and their meaning. We have a whole book in Etruscan, but no one can understand it. The key to the deciphering of ancient Egyptian was found in a brief chance inscription, the trilingual Rosetta stone, made for another purpose and never thought of at the time as being useful as a key. If the Etruscans, Egyptians, or other ancient peoples had planned to make a key for us, what would have been their procedure? If all connecting links had been removed, how could such a people have conveyed to us the pronunciation, grammar, and vocabulary of their language?

This question was propounded to the Smithsonian Institution with the result that it was decided that a mouth map would be necessary for the transmittal of pronunciation, diagrams for the conveying of grammatical categories, and the coinage of a list of "high-frequency English" words for the preservation of essential vocabulary.

The Rosetta stone was a key in that it gave a brief sample of translation. The deliberate scientific depicting of English of today for the people five thousand years from now will give adequate clues entirely independent of any furnishing of translation. It shows by a picture of the human mouth where each of the various sounds of speech comes from and with such clarity that the articulation can be re-enacted. It shows by cartoon-like diagrams the putting together of words. It shows by the development of a "high-frequency" vocabulary the vital constituents of the English of the present time.

THE SOUNDS OF ENGLISH

THE present English has thirty-three sounds. It is plain that the pronunciation cannot be transmitted to the people of the far future by traditional inherited spelling with its enormous irregularities. It is equally clear that if peculiar symbols be given to some of these thirty-three sounds, it will be bothersome for typewriter & newspaper equipment which has only the twenty-six letters. The letter *j* therefore is used instead of the inverted *e*, which last would require a special type, and digraphs, & in two instances trigraphs, are used instead of special vowel and consonant letters.

English has eight vowels ⌐or sounds whose hemming amounts to mere cavity-shape resonance⌐ and twenty-five consonants ⌐whose hemming amounts to closure, violent restriction, or closure followed by restriction⌐.

The vowels are all pronounced between the *k* and the *y* consonant positions, that is, between the back-of-the-tongue and the middle-of-the-tongue positions. The vowel with highest raised back of the tongue, that is, nearest to the *k* consonant position, is *u*; the vowel with the highest raised middle of the tongue, that is, nearest to the *y* consonant position, is *i*. *w* is here classified as a lip sound, though it is simultaneously a back-of-the-tongue sound. The other vowels have intermediate positions between the extreme *u* and *i*, *a* being the most open and *j* the most central positioned. The digraph *ae* stands for a vowel midway, perhaps, between *e* and *a*; *ao*, for a vowel midway, perhaps, between *a* and *o*. Vowels occur short and long. Since the letter *c* always stands for *k* or *s*, it is not needed for regular consonant duty and is here pressed into service as a long mark, being written as a silent character after a vowel where it is necessary to mark it as being long. Many vowels are long in English by simple rules, and in such instances the length sign *c* is not written. In fact, vowel length needs to be written in English only after *u* and *i*, to distinguish the long from the short varieties.

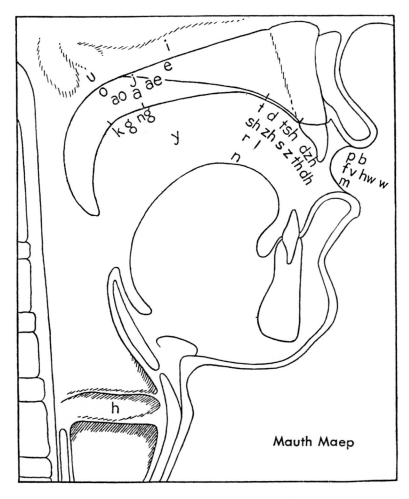

ILLUSTRATION 1, SHOWING EXACTLY WHERE EACH OF THE 33 SOUNDS OF 1938 ENGLISH IS FORMED IN THE ORAL CAVITY.

Vowel diphthongs are only four in number: *ui* [rare], *oi, au, ai*.

The complete closure consonants of simple form are *k, t, p*. Those which have the closure with the voice going simultaneously are *g, d, b*.

Restriction consonants of simple form are *h, sh, s, th, hw*. Those which have the restriction with voice going simultaneously are *y, zh, z, dh, l, r, w*.

Consonant diphthong of closure plus restriction of simple form is *tsh*. The same with the voice going simultaneously is *dzh*.

Consonants with the mouth completely hemmed but the nose open are *ng, n, m*.

The English language, like others, proceeds in syllables. Each syllable consists of a vowel or vowel diphthong, plus or minus consonant trimmings.

A word consisting of more than one syllable has one of its syllables, most commonly the next to the last, high and loud. Such a high and loud syllable is said to be accented. One-syllable words may or may not be high and loud, but it makes little difference to the understanding, whereas polysyllabic words are distorted if the highness and loudness are placed on the wrong syllable.

All sounds are made in the tract between the larynx and the lips. The points of articulation are the glottis of the larynx, the back of the tongue, the middle of the tongue, the front of the tongue, and the lips. Only *h* comes from the larynx. Only three consonants [*k, g, ng*] come from the back of the tongue. Only *y* comes from the middle of the tongue. By far the greatest number of consonants come from the flexible front of the tongue. That

[23]

is why "language," derived from the Latin word *lingua*, "tongue", is frequently called "tongue" in the various idioms of the world. From the front of the tongue come thirteen consonants [t, d, sh, ʐh, s, ʐ, th, dh, tsh, dʐh, l, r, n]. From the lips come five consonants [p, b, hw, w, m.]

Exercise on the Provenience of Vowels and Consonants

Vowels		Consonants			
put	pit	hit	den	dhen	pin
not	hui	kit	shin	tshin	bin
waotjr	boi	get	aeʐhur	dʐhin	faen
fadhjr	bau	sing	sin	letjr	hwen
bjrd	bai	yuc	ʐingk	rjn	wen
maen	mucn	ten	thin	nic	men
men	mict				

THE GRAMMAR OF ENGLISH

THE noun shows only two forms : singular, referring to one object, and plural, referring to two or more objects. This difference is shown by Illustration 2 which depicts the singular, "bird," as distinguished from the plural, "birds." A possessive case is the only remnant of earlier case formation and is formed like the plural by adding s, but distinguished orthographically by placing an apostrophe ['] before the added s in the singular and after it in the plural : "bird's," "birds'."

Singgyular aend Plucral—Singular and Plural.

bjrd   Illustration 2   **bjrdz**

[24]

The personal pronoun distinguishes three persons, see Illustration 3. The first person is the self of the speaking subject; the second person is the speaking subject addressed; the third person is the person neither originating the speech nor directly addressed. These three persons also have plurals: "I—we," "you—you," "he, she, it—they." It will be noticed that only in the third person singular is gender distinguished: "he," masculine animate; "she," feminine animate; "it," inanimate, also sometimes used when a lower animal is the object referred to, as: the sheep, it grazes.

The demonstrative pronouns have only two degrees of remoteness: "this" [here], and "that" [there]. The demonstrative adverbs "here" and "there" correspond.

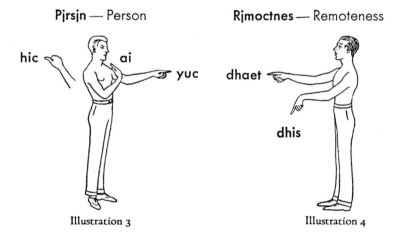

Pjrsjn — Person   Rjmoctnes — Remoteness

hic   ai   yuc   dhaet   dhis

Illustration 3   Illustration 4

Adjectives express permanent or acquired attributes of an object. They are often explained by giving the opposites, as in Illustration 5, where "young" and "old," "black" & "white," "short" & "tall" are contrasted.

[25]

Opjzits — Opposites

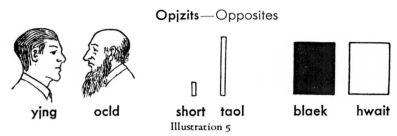

| yjng | ocld | short | taol | blaek | hwait |

Illustration 5

Adjectives have three degrees of comparison, as in Illustration 6, good being the positive, better indicating that good is excelled as one racer excels another, & best indicating that good is excelled as one racer excels all.

Kompaerisjn — Comparison

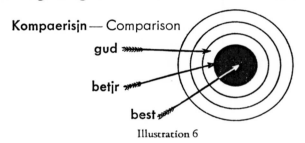

gud ⫸⫸⫸

betjr ⫸⫸⫸

best ⫸⫸

Illustration 6

Frequent verbs, that is, words denoting action or status, are shown graphically in Illustration 7, which gives: I lie, I sit, I stand, I walk, I run, I kick, I jump, I crawl, I climb, I descend.

ai lai   ai sit   ai staend   ai waok   ai rjn   ai kik

ai dzhjmp   ai kraol   ai klaim   ai djsend

Illustration 7

⟦ 26 ⟧

Tensez— Tenses

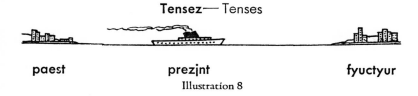

paest   prezjnt   fyuctyur

Illustration 8

The verb has three main tenses or times, well shown
in Illustration 8, where the steamer in mid-water is the
present, the port left behind indicates the past, and the
port which is the destination is the future of the action.

The verb in 1938 English has still another expression:
it is principal or subordinate. Illustration 9 shows the
sentence: "Running he aimed," in which "aimed" is the
principal verb and "running" the subordinate.

Sjbordinecshjn
— Subordination

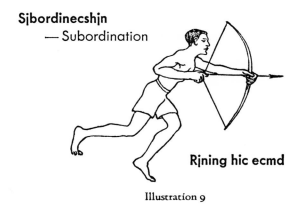

Rjning hic ecmd

Illustration 9

To illustrate these elements of English grammar, and
as an exercise in 1938 English pronunciation, we give
next a little story, The Fable of the Northwind and the
Sun, written first in neo-phonetic spelling, followed by
the ordinary English spelling.

[27]

DHJ FECBJL JV DHJ NORTHWIND AEND DHJ SJN

The Fable of the Northwind and the Sun

Dhj Northwind aend dhj Sjn wjr dispyucting whitsh woz dhj stronggjr, hwen j traevjljr kecm jlong raepd in j worm klock. Dhec jgricd dhaet dhj wjn huc fjrst mecd dhj traevjljr teck of hiz klock shud bic konsidjrd stronggjr dhaen dhj jdhjr. Dhen dhj Northwind bluc widh aol hiz mait, bjt dhj mocr hic bluc, dhj mocr klocsli did dhj traevjljr focld hiz klock jraund him, aend aet laest dhj Northwind gecv jp dhj jtempt. Dhen dhj Sjn shocn aut wormli, aend imicdijtli dhj traevjljr tuk of hiz klock; aend soc dhj Northwind woz jblaidzhd tj konfes dhaet dhj Sjn woz dhj stronggjr jv dhj tuc.

The Northwind and the Sun were disputing which was the stronger, when a traveler came along wrapped in a warm cloak. They agreed that the one who first made the traveler take off his cloak should be considered stronger than the other. Then the Northwind blew with all his might, but the more he blew, the more closely did the traveler fold his cloak around him; and at last the Northwind gave up the attempt. Then the Sun shone out warmly, and immediately the traveler took off his cloak.; and so the Northwind was obliged to confess that the Sun was the stronger of the two.

As a further aid to translation and pronunciation, we have enclosed in the Time Capsule reproductions of this simply worded fable in twenty-five languages. We follow, here, with the English vocabulary most used in 1938—the thousand words most essential to our daily speech and thought. Taking a suggestion from the electrical engineers, we have named the vocabulary "High-frequency English." We attach, also, two more illustrations, one showing an exterior view of 1938 life, the other an interior view, with common terms indicated.

[28]

VOCABULARY OF HIGH-FREQUENCY ENGLISH

The Thousand Most-used Words of English in Neo-phonetic Spelling

(Editor's Note—Dr. Harrington has compiled this list follow-ing detailed statistical study of newspapers, magazines, books of varying calibre and purpose, and most especially the silent stream of thought, the words spoken every day, and the words most frequently used on the radio and recorded by phonograph. The list has been further improved by comparison with vocabu-laries given in the various books used for learning foreign lan-guages, and especially with the statistical work of Professor Curme in determining the commonest words of German).

Illustration 10

Autdocr Necmz (Outdoor Names)
1 smock (smoke)   2 skai (sky)   3 klaud (cloud)   4 barn (barn)
5 hecstaek (haystack) 6 tric (tree) 7 wudz (woods) 8 haus (house)
9 kau (cow)   1 0 ficld (field)   1 1 fens (fence)   1 2 rocd (road)
13 hors (horse)   1 4 aotomobicl (automobile)

[29]

Illustration 11

Indocr Necmz (Indoor Names)

1 pot (pot)   2 tecbjl (table)   3 bocl (bowl)   4 ridzhpocl (ridgepole)
5 tshimni (chimney)   6 fairplecs (fireplace)   7 naif (knife)   8 fair (fire)
9 rjg (rug)   10 tshaer (chair)   11 bed (bed)   12 waol (wall)
13 docr (door)   14 windoc (window)   15 raeftjr (rafter)   16 gjn (gun)
17 aeks (axe)   18 kaet (cat)

a

aeftjr (after)   aeks (axe)   ai (I, eye)   aidicj (idea)   aijrn (iron)
ailjnd (island)   ais (ice)   aekjmpjni (accompany)   aekt (act)
aem (am)   aend (and)   aengkjl (ankle)   aenimjl (animal)
aenjdhjr (another)   aensjr (answer)   aent (aunt)   aepjl (apple)
aer (air)   aesk (ask)   aet (at)   aez (as)   aol (all)   aolredi (already)
aolwecz (always)   aot (ought)   ar (are)   arm (arm)   art (art)
aut (out)   aur (our)   awr (hour)

b

baed (bad)   baeg (bag)   baek (back)   baengk (bank)   baer (bear)
baeth (bath)   bai (buy, by)   baind (bind)   bait (bite)   baol (ball)
baot (bought)   barn (barn)   bau (bow)   baujlz (bowels)   baund (bound)
becbi (baby)   becdh (bathe)   beck (bake)   becs (base)   bed (bed)
beg (beg)   bel (bell)   beli (belly)   beri (bury, berry)   best (best)
betjr (better)   bic (be, bee)   bicf (beef)   bicnz (beans)
bict (beat, beet),   big (big)   bilding (building)   bin (been)   bitjr (bitter)
bizi (busy)   bizniz (business)   bjfocr (before)   bjgin (begin)
bjhaind (behind)   bjkazo (because)   bjket (bucket)   bjkjm (become)
bjlicv (believe)   bjloc (below)   bjrd (bird)   bjrth (birth)   bjsaid (beside)
bjt (but, butt)   bjtjr (butter)   bird (beard)   bjrn (burn)   bjrst (burst)
bjtjn (button)   bjtwicn (between)   blaek (black)   blaenket (blanket)
blaind (blind)   blecd (blade)   blecm (blame)   blecz (blaze)   bljd (blood)
bloc (blow)   bluc (blue)   bocld (bold)   bocn (bone)   bocr (bore)
bocrd (board)   boct (boat)   bodi (body)   boi (boy)   bocl (bowl)
boks (box)   born (born)   boroc (borrow)   botjl (bottle)   botjm (bottom)
brait (bright)   brau (brow)   braun (brown)   breck (break, brake)
brecn (brain)   brecv (brave)   bred (bread, bred)   brest (breast)
breth (breath)   bridzh (bridge)   brik (brick)   bring (bring)
brjdhjr (brother)   brjsh (brush)   brock (broke)   brockjn (broken)
buk (book)   bynctiful (beautiful)

d

daens (dance)   daotjr (daughter)   dark (dark)   daun (down)
daut (doubt)   dec (day)   ded (dead)   def (deaf)   det (debt)   deth (death)
dhaen (than)   dhaet (that)   dhec (they)   dhecr (their, there)   dhem (them)
dhen (then)   dhis (this)   dhicz (these)   dhj (the)   dhoc (though)
dhocz (those)   dicl (deal)   dicp (deep)   dicr (dear, deer)   did (did)
difjrjnt (different)   dig (dig)   dim (dim)   dish (dish)   djl (dull)
djn (done, dun)   djrt (dirt)   djrti (dirty)   djst (dust)   djz (does)
docr (door)   dog (dog)   doktjr (doctor)   doljr (dollar)   draeg (drag)
drai (dry)   draiv (drive)   drao (draw)   draun (drown)   dres (dress)
dringk (drink)   drjngk (drunk)   drop (drop)   dzhob (job)   dzhoin (join)
dzhjdzh (judge)   dzhjmp (jump)   duc (do)

e

ecbjl (able)   eck (ache)   ecm (aim)   ect (eight, ate)   ecti (eighty)
ecticn (eighteen)   edzh (edge)   eg (egg)   empti (empty)   end (end)
enemi (enemy)   eni (any)   entjr (enter)   evjr (ever)   evri (every)

f

fadhjr (father) faekt (fact) faest (fast) faet (fat) fain (fine) faind (find)
fair (fire)   fait (fight)   faiv (five)   faol (fall)   far (far)   farm (farm)
fecs (face) fedhjr (feather) fel (fell) fens (fence) ficld (field) ficl (feel)
ficr (fear)   ficst (feast)   fifti (fifty)   fifticn (fifteen)   fiks (fix)
finggjr (finger) finish (finish) fish (fish) fjrst (first) flaeg (flag) flaet (flat)
flai (fly)   flaur (flower, flour)   fling (fling)   flocn (flown)   flocr (floor)
floct (float)   fluc (flue,   flew, flu)   focld (fold)   focr (four)
focrticn (fourteen)   fols (false)   for (for)   fork (fork)   form (form)
fors (force) forti (forty) forwjrd (forward) frend (friend) fresh (fresh)
fric (free)   frjm (from)   frjnt (front)   fruct (fruit)   fucd (food)   fucl (fool)
fuclish (foolish)   ful (full)   fut (foot)   fyuc (few)   fyuctyur (future)

g

gaedhjr (gather)   gaes (gas)   gaid (guide)   gaon (gone)   gardjn (garden)
get (get)   gecv (gave)   giv (give)   gilti (guilty)   gjn (gun)
gjrl (girl)   gjts (guts)   glaed (glad)   gljv (glove)   glaes (glass)   goc (go)
gocld (gold)   goct (goat)   got (got)   graes (grass)   grec (gray)
grecp (grape)   grect (great)   gricn (green)   grip (grip)   groc (grow)
gud (good)   gudbai (good-bye)

h

haef (half) haemjr (hammer) haend (hand) haendkjrtshif (handkerchief)
haeng (hang)   haepi (happy)   haer(hair)   haet (hat)   haev (have)
haez (has) haed (had) hai (high) haid (hide) hard (hard) hart (heart)
hau (how)   haus (house)   hect (hate)   hed (head)   held (held)
helth (health)   hic (he)   hicl (heel, heal)   hip (hip)   hicr (hear, here)
hict (heat)   hidjn (hidden)   hil (hill)   him (him)   hit (hit)   hiz (his)
hjndred (hundred)   hjnggjr (hunger)   hjnggri (hungry)   hjnt (hunt)
hjr (her) hjrt (hurt) hjzbjnd (husband) hocl (hole, whole) hocld (hold)

hocp (hope)   holoc (hollow)   hop (hop)   horn (horn)   hors (horse)
hot (hot)   huc (who)   hucm (whom)   hucz (whose)   huf (hoof)
huk (hook)   hwaer (where, wear, ware)   hwai (why)   hwail (while)
hwait (white)   hwedhjr (whether)   hwen (when)   hwicl (wheel)
hwiskjrz (whiskers)   hwiski (whiskey)   hwisjl (whistle)   hwip (whip)
hwitsh (which)   hwjt (what)

i

icr (ear)   icst (east)   ict (eat)   icvn (even)   icvning (evening)   if (if)
il (ill)   in (in)   ingk (ink)   it (it)   its (its)   iz (is)

j

j (a)   jbjv (above)   jdhjr (other)   jfrecd (afraid)   jgen (again)
jgenst (against)   jgoc (ago)   jkaunt (account)   jksept (except)
jkros (across)   jlaiv (alive)   jlektrik (electric)   jlevjn (eleven)
jmjng (among)   jn (an)   jndjr (under)   jndjrstaend (understand)
jnjf (enough)   jnkjl (uncle)   jntil (until)   jp (up)   jpjr (upper)
jraund (around)   jrli (early)   jrn (earn)   jrth (earth)   js (us)   jv (of)
jvjn (oven)   jwec (away)   jweck (awake)

k

kaebedzh (cabbage)   kaef (calf)   kaen (can)   kaer (care)   kaeri (carry)
kaet (cat)   kaetjl (cattle)   kaetsh (catch)   kaind (kind)   kaof (cough)
kaol (call)   kaot (caught)   kar (car)   kard (card)   kau (cow)
kaunt (count)   keck (cake)   kecm (came)   kept (kept)   ketjl (kettle)
kic (key)   kik (kick)   kicp (keep)   kil (kill)   king (king)   kis (kiss)
kraek (crack)   krai (cry)   kreczi (crazy)   kraim (crime)   krjsh (crush)
kruked (crooked)   kjmpaenyjn (companion)   kjntri (country)   kjp (cup)
kjt (cut)   klaim (climb)   klaud (cloud)   klicn (clean)   klicr (clear)
klocs (close)   klok (clock)   klocz (close)   kloth (cloth)   kocld (cold)
kocm (comb)   kocrn (corn)   koct (coat)   kofi (coffee)   koljr (collar)
kopi (copy)   kopjr (copper)   kornjr (corner)   kost (cost)
kotjn (cotton)   kucl (cool)   kud (could)   kukd (cooked)   kuk (cook)
kwaijt (quiet)   kwait (quite)   kwestshjn (question)   kwicn (queen)
kwik (quick)   kwoliti (quality)   kworel (quarrel)   kyucr (cure)

l

lec (lay)   laef (laugh)   laend (land)   laengwedzh (language)
laemp (lamp)   laest (last)   lai (lie, lye)   laif (life)   laijn (lion)
laik (like)   lain (line)   lait (light)   lao (law)   lecdi (lady)   leck (lake)
lecm (lame)   lect (late)   led (lead, led)   leczi (lazy)   left (left)   leg (leg)
les (less)   let (let)   letjr (letter)   levjl (level)   licd (lead)   licf (leaf)
licn (lean)   licst (least)   licv (leave)   lift (lift)   lip (lip)   list (list)
litjl (little)   liv (live)   ljk (luck)   ljmp (lump)   ljv (love)   ljrn (learn)
loc (low)   locd (load)   locjr (lower)   lok (lock)   long (long)
los (loss)   lost (lost)   lots (lots)   lucs (loose)   luk (look)   lucz (lose)

m

maed (mad)   maen (man)   maeri (marry)   maetjr (matter)   maetsh (match)
mai (my)   mait (might)   mark (mark)   mauntjn (mountain)
maus (mouse)   mauth (mouth)   mec (may)   mecbic (maybe)
mecd (made, maid)   meck (make)   medisin (medicine)   melt (melt)
men (men)   meni (many)   mesh (mesh)   met (met)   metjl (metal)
mezhur (measure)   mic (me)   mjd (mud)   mjdhjr (mother)   mjni (money)
mjnth (month)   mjsh (mush)   mjshicn (machine)   mjst (must)
mjtsh (much)   micl (meal)   micn (mean)   mict (meet, meat)
midjl (middle)   milk (milk)   mis (miss)   mocr (more)   mocst (most)
morning (morning)   mucn (moon)   mucv (move)

n

naif (knife)   nain (nine)   nainticn (nineteen)   nainti (ninety)
nais (nice)   nait (night)   nau (now)   necbjr (neighbor)   necl (nail)
necm (name)   necshjn (nation)   nefyu (nephew)   nek (neck)
nektai (necktie)   nic (knee)   nicd (need)   nicdjl (needle)   nicr (near)
nies (niece)   njmbjr (number)   njn (none)   njrv (nerve)   njthing (nothing)
njt (nut)   noc (no)   noct (note)   nocz (nose)   noiz (noise)   nok (knock)
north (north)   not (not, knot)   nucn (noon)   nyuc (new)   nyucz (news)

o

ocld (old)   ocn (own)   ocnli (only)   ocvjr (over)   of (off)   ofis (office)
ofjn (often)   ofjr (offer)   oil (oil)   olsoc (also)   on (on)   opjzit (opposite)
or (or)   ordjr (order)   ocpjn (open)

p

paek (pack)   paents (pants)   paes (pass)   paest (past)   pai (pie)
part (part)   paudjr (powder)   paujr (power)   paund (pound)
pec (pay)   pecn (pain)   pecnt (paint)   pecpjr (paper)   pecst (paste)
pen (pen)   picl (peel, peal)   picpjl (people)   pics (piece, peace)
        pictsh (peach)   pig (pig)   pin (pin)   pjmp (pump)
pjrhaeps (perhaps)   pjrpjs (purpose)   pjrsjn (person)   pjtecto (potato)
plaent (plant)   plau (plow)   plec (play)   plecn (plain, plane)
plecs (place)   plect (plate, plait)   plezhur (pleasure)   plicz (please)
point (point)   poket (pocket)   pot (pot)   praud (proud)   prec (pray)
precz (praise)   pres (press)   prezjnt (present)   print (print)
prucf (proof)   prucv (prove)   pruti (pretty)   pucr (poor)   pul (pull)
        push (push)   put (put)   pyucr (pure)

r

raebit (rabbit)   raen (ran)   raer (rare)   raet (rat)   raid (ride)
rais (rice, rise)   rait (write, right)   raiz (rise)   rao (raw)   raund (round)
rec (ray)   recdioc (radio)   recn (rain, reign)   recndzh (range)
rect (rate)   recz (raise)   red (red)   redi (ready)   rent (rent)
rest (rest)   ricd (read)   rictsh (reach)   riczijn (reason)   ring (ring)
rip (rip)   ritjn (written)   ritsh (rich)   rivjr (river)   rjb (rub)
rjf (rough)   rjmecn (remain)   rjn (run)   rocd (road)   rocl (roll, role)
rocz (rose)   rok (rock)   rong (wrong)   rot (rot)   rotjn (rotten)
rucl (rule)   ruf (roof)   rum (room)   rut (root)   ryucl (rule)

s

saed (sad) saek (sack) saend (sand) saet (sat) said (side) sain (sign)
sait (sight, site)   sao (saw)   saujr (sour)   saund (sound)   sauth (south)
sec (say)   secf (safe)   secm (same)   secv (save)   sed (said)
sekjnd (second)   sel (sell)   self (self)   send (send)   sens (sense)
sent (cent, sent)   set (set)   seventicn (seventeen)   sevjn (seven)
sevjnti (seventy)   shaedoc (shadow)   shael (shall)   shain (shine)
sharp (sharp) sheck (shake) shecm (shame) shecv (shave) shel (shell)
shic (she)   shicp (sheep)   shicr (shear)   shict (sheet   )ship (ship)
shjrt (shirt)   shjt (shut)   shoc (show)   short (short)   shuc (shoe)
shucr (sure)   shuct (shoot)   shud (should)   shugjr (sugar)   sic (sea, see)

[35]

sicd (seed)   sicm (seem)   sicn (scene, seen)   sict (seat)   sik (sick)   siks (six)
siksti (sixty)   siksticn (sixteen)   sili (silly)   silvjr (silver)   singk (sink)
sistjr (sister)   sit (sit)   siti (city)   sizjrz (scissors)   sjdjn (sudden)
sjfjr (suffer)   sjk (suck)   sjm (some)   (sjmjr (summer)
sjmthing (something)   sjn (sun, son)   sjrv (serve)   sjtsh (such)
skai (sky)   skecl (scale)   skin (skin)   skjrt (skirt)   skocld (scold)
skraetsh (scratch)   skruc (screw)   skucl (school)   skwaer (square)
skwicz (squeeze)   slaotjr (slaughter)   slicp (sleep)   slicpi (sleepy)
sling (sling)   slip (slip)   sloc (slow)   smail (smile)   smaol (small)
smart (smart)   smel (smell)   smock (smoke)   smucdh (smooth)
sneck (snake)   snicz (sneeze)   snoc (snow)   snocr (snore)   soc (so)
socldzhjr (soldier)   socp (soap)   soft (soft)   soc (sew, sow, so)
socl (soul)   sok (sock)   solti (salty)   solt (salt)   song (song)
sort (sort)   spend (spend)   spick (speak)   spictsh (speech)   spil (spill)
spin (spin)   spit (spit)   split (split)   spoil (spoil)   spraut (sprout)
spring (spring)   staemp (stamp) staend (stand)   staerz (stairs)   star (star)
start (start)   stec (stay)   steck (stake, steak)   step (step)
sticl (steal, steel)   sticm (steam)   stif (stiff)   stik (stick)   stiki (sticky)
stil (still)   stingk (stink)   stitsh (stitch)   stjdi (study)   stocn (stone)
stocr (store)   stocri (story)   stocv (stove)   stop (stop)   storm (storm)
straik (strike)   straipd (striped)   strecn (strain)   strecndzh (strange)
strect (straight, strait)   stretsh (stretch)   strict (street)   string (string)
strip (strip)   strong (strong)   stucpid (stupid)   sucp (soup)   sun (soon)
swel (swell)   swet (sweat)   swicp (sweep)   swict (sweet)   swim (swim)
      swoloc (swallow)   swop (swap)   syuct (suit)

t

taeks (tax)   taer (tear)   taim (time)   taird (tired)   tait (tight)
taok (talk)   taol (tall)   taot (taught)   taun (town)   tecbjl (table)
teck (take)   teckjn (taken)   tecl (tail, tale)   tecm (tame)
tecst (taste)   tel (tell)   ten (ten)   thaot (thought)
thauzjnd (thousand)   thief (thief)   thik (thick)   thin (thin)
thing (thing)   thingk (think)   thjm (thumb)   thjndjr (thunder)
thred (thread)   throc (throw)   thric (three)   thjrst (thirst)
thjrsti (thirsty)   thjrti (thirty)   thjrticn (thirteen)   thorn (thorn)
throc (throw)   throct (throat)   thruc (through)   tic (tea)   tictsh (teach)
til (till)   tin (tin)   tip (tip)   tjb (tub)   tjdec (today)   tjgedhjr (together)
tjmoroc (tomorrow)   tjng (tongue)   tjrn (turn)   tjtsh (touch)   toc (toe)

tocld (told)   top (top)   torn (torn)   towjrdz (towards)   trai (try)
trip (trip)   truc (true)   tshaens (chance)   tshaer (chair)
tshaild (child)   tshecs (chase)   tsheindzh (change)   tshick (cheek)
tshicf (chief)   tshicp (cheap)   tshimni (chimney)   tshin (chin)
tshicz (cheese)   tshecn (chain)   tshock (choke)   tshuc (chew)
tshucz (choose) tuc (to, two) tucth (tooth) tuk (took) twelv (twelve)
twenti (twenty)   twenti-faiv (twenty-five)   twenti-wjn (twenty-one)
twist (twist)

V

vain (vine)   veri (very)   vesjl (vessel)

W

waid (wide)   waif (wife)   waild (wild)   wain (wine)   waind (wind)
waiz (wise)   waok (walk)   waol (wall)   waotjr (water)
wec (way, weigh)   wecst (waist)   wecdzhez (wages)
weck (wake)   wect (wait, weight)   wecv (wave)   wedhjr (weather)
wel (well)   went (went)   west (west)   wet (wet)   wic (we)
wick (weak)   wicp (weep)   widhin (within)   widh (with)
widhaut (without)   wil (will)   windoc (window)   wind (wind)
wing (wing)   wintjr (winter)   wish (wish) wjn (one)   wjns (once)
wjr (were)   wjrd (word)   wjrk (work)   wjrld (world)
wjrs (worse)   wjrst (worst)   wjrm (worm)   wont (want)   wor (war)
worm (warm)   wosh (wash)   watsh (watch)   woz (was)
wud (would, wood)   wudz (woods)   wul (wool)   wumen (women)
wumjn (woman)

Y

yaon (yawn)   yel (yell)   yeloc (yellow)   yes (yes)
yestjrdec (yesterday)   yet (yet)   yicr (year)   yjng (young)
yocr (your)   yuc (you)   yucs (use)   yucz (use)

Units of Linear Measurement

ENGLISH SYSTEM

<----------1 INCH----------->

12 inches = 1 foot
3 feet = 1 yard
5,280 feet = 1 mile
1 inch = 2.54 centimeters

METRIC SYSTEM

<----------->
1 CENTIMETER

1 centimeter = 10 millimeters
100 centimeters = 1 meter
1000 meters = 1 kilometer
1 centimeter = .3937 inch

1 meter is equal to 1,553,164.13 wave
lengths of red cadmium light

SEEKING METALLIC SUBSTANCES BENEATH THE GROUND

Sherwin Kelly

CHAIRMAN, COMMITTEE ON GEOPHYSICAL METHODS OF
EXPLORATION, AMERICAN INSTITUTE OF MINING
AND METALLURGICAL ENGINEERS

THOUGH in all probability methods more sensitive than any we have today will be employed in the future to seek for metallic bodies beneath the earth, it is possible, too, that this will become a lost art. It is therefore suggested that the Time Capsule may be discovered by detecting the secondary electromagnetic field induced in it by a strong primary electrical field created at the surface of the ground.

Construct a loop some ten feet in diameter, composed of several turns of well-insulated wire, fashioned in such a manner that it can be moved systematically over the area within which the Capsule is believed to lie. While the loop stands vertically, pass through it an alternating current of 1,000 to 5,000 cycles, using a power source of 200 watts. The primary electromagnetic field thus set up around the loop will intersect any metallic material in the vicinity, such as the Capsule, and will induce in it a secondary current. This current will produce a secondary electromagnetic field such as will distort the primary field of the "energizing" loop. This distortion, properly interpreted, will indicate the location of the Capsule.

To investigate this phenomenon, construct a second, smaller coil, approximately a foot in diameter, made up of a large number of turns of insulated wire. To the coil

[39]

should be connected an amplifier which in turn is connected to some type of current indicator, such as a galvanometer or telephone receiver. Some means should be provided for accurately measuring the strike or direction of the coil in the horizontal plane, as well as its dip or deviation from the vertical position. On level ground, where there is nothing to distort the primary field, the current generated in the small, or pickup coil will be at a minimum [that is, produce the least deflection of the galvanometer needle or the least sound in the telephone receiver] when its plane is perpendicular to that of the large coil. Conversely, the maximum current will be observed when the two coils are in the same plane. It is well to take both observations as a checkup before beginning the search for the Capsule. If the instrument is working properly, the positions of minimum and maximum current in the pickup coil should be at right angles to each other.

In exploring for the Capsule, observations may be made with the pickup coil in two ways.

First: Take measurements in the plane of the energizing loop, moving farther and farther away from it in short stages of five or ten feet. Do not work too close to the energizing loop. If during this survey the pickup coil passes over buried metallic material it will be noted that the positions of the coil do not correspond to those described for an undistorted field. The divergence from the normal dip will be at a maximum over the hidden body, whereas the deviation from the normal strike will increase as the metallic substance is approached, reverse to a maximum in the opposite direction as the spot is passed over, and then decrease as the coil moves farther away.

Second: Take readings along lines at right angles to the measurements suggested in the first method above. These readings should be taken approximately five to ten feet apart, extending fifty to one hundred feet each side of the plane of the energizing coil. The lines of observation should cross the first line every five feet. Observe the position of maximum current in the pickup coil. In an undisturbed field the coil should stand vertically. As the metallic body is approached the position of maximum current in the pickup will stand at an angle from the vertical, and its plane will point roughly to the buried metallic mass. When it passes over the Capsule, the plane of maximum current of the pickup coil will again become vertical. As the coil passes beyond, it will reverse & point in the opposite direction. The strike will undergo a maximum deviation from its normal position as the Capsule is passed.

By a combination of these two methods it should be possible to locate the position of the Time Capsule within a few feet. However, if any other metallic objects lie within the area, they may also give indications. In our day we know of no way to distinguish by geophysical prospecting between different types of metallic substances when they are concealed beneath the ground.

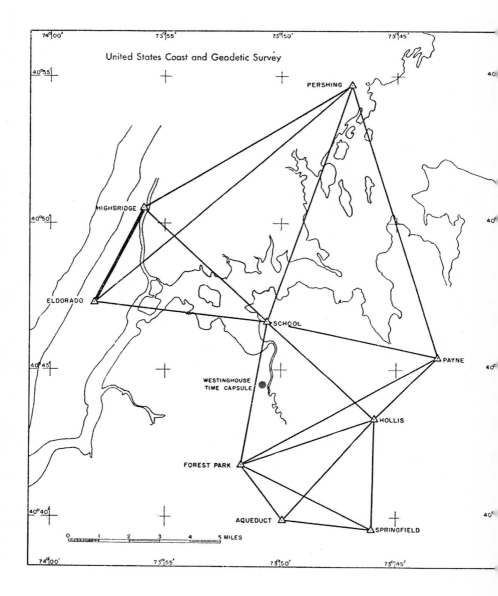

DETERMINATION OF LATITUDE AND LONGITUDE

COMMANDER C. L. GARNER

CHIEF, DIVISION OF GEODESY

UNITED STATES COAST AND GEODETIC SURVEY

C. H. SWICK

CHIEF, SECTION OF GRAVITY AND ASTRONOMY, DIVISION OF

GEODESY, UNITED STATES COAST AND GEODETIC SURVEY

THE geodetic latitude and longitude of the Time Capsule has been determined by the United States Coast and Geodetic Survey by means of precise triangulation measurements from nearby stations of an extensive rigid Federal net comprising more than fifty thousand stations distributed over the United States. The net extends from the Atlantic to the Pacific Ocean, across the entire North American continent, and is included between latitudes 25° and 49° north of the Equator, and longitudes 68° and 125° west from Greenwich, England. The net has been extended into Canada and Mexico by the two countries involved & the datum on which it is based is called the North American Datum of 1927.

The accompanying sketch shows the first-order stations of the national net in the general vicinity of the Time Capsule. It should be noted that the latitude and longitude furnished for the Capsule are geodetic & may differ by as much as five seconds or more from the latitude and longitude determined by astronomical observations alone. This is due to deflections of the plumb line from the vertical, which are caused by the attraction of mountain masses or other topographic features & by the

[43]

unequal distribution of mass in the crust of the earth. These defleᔸions can be determined only by comparison of geodetic and astronomic latitudes and longitudes at identical or nearly identical stations. No astronomic observations have been made at the point above the Capsule. However, at station Forest Park, shown on the sketch, observations for astronomical longitude, latitude, and azimuth have been made and furnish the following comparison:

Geodetic latitude	40° 41' 49".518
Astronomic latitude	40° 41' 42".38
Geodetic longitude	73° 51' 43".966
Astronomic longitude	73° 51' 42".30
Geodetic azimuth to station School	190° 07' 54".20
Astronomic azimuth to station School	190° 07' 55".28

Any operations for locating the Capsule by astronomical means should be started as nearly as possible at station Forest Park. After this point has been located the measurement of a base line for the determination of distances and the extension of triangulation to the position of the Time Capsule can be done without difficulty.

A study of conditions in and around New York City would indicate that there will be no chance five thousand years from now of recovering any of the triangulation stations shown on the sketch except possibly Forest Park. This station is located in Forest Park, Borough of Queens, New York City, six meters north of Park Lane and 70 meters east of the easterly line of Forest Parkway [extended]. It is marked by a cross in a granite post 0.15 meter square and 0.6 meter long embedded in a mass of concrete 0.9 meter square and 1.2 meters deep.

[44]

It should be noted that according to the present system in use in this country, the distance from the Equator
to either pole is divided into 90 degrees [°] and each degree is equal to 60 minutes ['] or 3600 seconds ["]. The
unit of length is the meter [3.28083 feet]. At station Forest Park one second of latitude equals 30.846 meters,
and one minute equals 1850.77 meters.

A more detailed description of the triangulation net
of the United States and of the North American Datum
of 1927 will be found in the Capsule.

MESSAGES FOR THE FUTURE FROM
NOTED MEN OF OUR TIME

IN ORDER that peoples who live long after us may see
our world somewhat as we see it, and understand at
least some of the viewpoints of our contemporary world,
three men, chosen for their high reputation among us,
have summed up in their own words the strengths and
weaknesses of our age, pointed out the discernible trends
of human history, & envisioned something of the future.
The messages follow.

[45]

THE MESSAGE OF DR. ROBERT A. MILLIKAN

AT this moment, August 22, 1938, the principles of representative ballot government, such as are represented by the governments of the Anglo-Saxon, French, and Scandinavian countries, are in deadly conflict with the principles of despotism, which up to two centuries ago had controlled the destiny of man throughout practically the whole of recorded history. If the rational, scientific, progressive principles win out in this struggle there is a possibility of a warless, golden age ahead for mankind. If the reactionary principles of despotism triumph now and in the future, the future history of mankind will repeat the sad story of war and oppression as in the past.

Robert A. Millikan.

ROBERT A. MILLIKAN [1868-   ], physicist, isolated and measured the ultimate electric unit, the electron; contributed greatly to other fields of research, especially photoelectric phenomena and cosmic rays; awarded Nobel Prize in physics, 1923; chairman, Executive Council, California Institute of Technology, Pasadena, California.

[46]

The Message of Dr. Thomas Mann

WE know now that the idea of the future as a "better world" was a fallacy of the doctrine of progress. The hopes we center on you, citizens of the future, are in no way exaggerated. In broad outline, you will actually resemble us very much as we resemble those who lived a thousand, or five thousand, years ago. Among you too the spirit will fare badly—it should never fare too well on this earth, otherwise men would need it no longer. That optimistic conception of the future is a projection into time of an endeavor which does not belong to the temporal world, the endeavor on the part of man to approximate to his idea of himself, the humanization of man. What we, in this year of Our Lord 1938, understand by the term "culture"—a notion held in small esteem today by certain nations of the western world—is simply this endeavor. What we call the spirit is identical with it, too. Brothers of the future, united with us in the spirit and in this endeavor, we send our greetings.

THOMAS MANN [1875-   ], German novelist & essayist; awarded Nobel Prize in literature, 1929. Now living in the United States.

[47]

The Message of Dr. Albert Einstein

In unserer Zeit gibt es viele erfindungsreiche Köpfe, deren Erfindungen unser Leben in hohem Masse erleichtern könnten. Wir durchqueren die Meere mit Maschinenkraft und benutzen die letztere auch, um die Menschen von aller anstrengenden Muskelarbeit zu befreien. Wir haben fliegen gelernt und senden uns bequem alle Nachrichten über die ganze Erde durch elektrische Wellen. Aber die Produktion und Verteilung der Güter ist völlig unorganisiert, so daß jeder in der Angst leben muß, aus dem Kreislauf der Wirtschaft ausgeschaltet zu werden und an allem Mangel zu leiden. Ausserdem töten einander die Menschen, die in verschiedenen Ländern wohnen, in unregelmäßigen Zeitabschnitten, so daß auch aus diesem Grunde alle in Furcht und Schrecken leben, welche sich irgendwie über die Zukunft Gedanken machen. Alles hängt damit zusammen, daß die Intelligenz und Charakter-Bildung der Massen unvergleichlich tiefer steht als die entsprechenden Eigenschaften der wenigen, die für die Gesamtheit Wertvolles hervorbringen.

Hoffentlich liest das spätere Geschlecht diese Konstatierungen mit dem Gefühl stolzer und berechtigter Überlegenheit.

A. Einstein.

Albert Einstein [1879-   ], theoretical physicist; discoverer and exponent of the theory of relativity; life member of the Institute for Advanced Study, Princeton, New Jersey.

AUTHORIZED ENGLISH TRANSLATION

Herewith follows Dr. Einstein's message in authorized English translation:

OUR time is rich in inventive minds, the inventions of which could facilitate our lives considerably. We are crossing the seas by power and utilize power also in order to relieve humanity from all tiring muscular work. We have learned to fly and we are able to send messages and news without any difficulty over the entire world through electric waves.

However, the production and distribution of commodities is entirely unorganized so that everybody must live in fear of being eliminated from the economic cycle, in this way suffering for the want of everything. Furthermore, people living in different countries kill each other at irregular time intervals, so that also for this reason any one who thinks about the future must live in fear and terror. This is due to the fact that the intelligence & character of the masses are incomparably lower than the intelligence and character of the few who produce something valuable for the community.

I trust that posterity will read these statements with a feeling of proud and justified superiority.

ACKNOWLEDGMENTS

A MONG the scientists, scholars and other persons of special skills of our time, several hundred have co-operated with men of the Westinghouse Electric & Manufacturing Company to shape the Time Capsule, determine its contents, and guide the writing and making of this book. To all of them we give acknowledgment and gratitude, and especially to the following:

JOHN ARCHER, Superintendent of the Printing Office, The New York Public Library.

HOWARD BLAKESLEE, Science Editor, The Associated Press.

ALLYN BUTTERFIELD, Editor, RKO-Pathe News, Inc.

LAURENCE V. COLEMAN, Director, American Museums Association.

L. O. COLBERT, REAR ADMIRAL, Director, U. S. Coast and Geodetic Survey.

R. D. W. CONNOR, Archivist of the United States.

ROBERT TREAT CRANE, Director, Social Science Research Council.

WATSON DAVIS, Director, Science Service.

DAVID DIETZ, Science Editor, Scripps-Howard Newspapers.

ALBERT EINSTEIN, Institute for Advanced Study.

ALDEN H. EMERY, American Chemical Society.

MORRIS FISHBEIN, M.D., Editor, Journal of the American Medical Association.

LESTER D. GARDNER, Secretary, Institute of the Aeronautical Sciences.

C. L. GARNER, COMMANDER, Chief of Division of Geodesy, U. S. Coast and Geodetic Survey.

G. LEONARD GOLD, Prestige Book Company.

FREDERIC W. GOUDY, Typographer, Printer and Type Designer.

JOHN P. HARRINGTON, Bureau of Ethnology, Smithsonian Institution.

MAURICE A. HECHT, LIEUTENANT, U.S. Coast and Geodetic Survey.

J. F. HELLWEG, CAPTAIN [Retired], U. S. N., Director, U. S. Naval Observatory.

[50]

HARRISON E. HOWE, Editor, Industrial & Engineering Chemistry.

E. EASTMAN IRVINE, Editor, World Almanac.

JOTHAM JOHNSON, Classical Weekly, University of Pittsburgh.

SHERWIN KELLY, Chairman, Committee on Geophysical Methods of Exploration, American Institute of Mining and Metallurgical Engineers.

A. V. KIDDER, Chairman, Division of Historical Research, Carnegie Institution of Washington.

A. E. KIMBERLY, Chief, Division of Repair and Preservation, The National Archives.

CUTHBERT LEE, Director, American Documentation Institute.

HARRY M. LYDENBERG, Director, The New York Public Library.

F. D. McHUGH, Managing Editor, Scientific American.

THOMAS MANN, Novelist and Essayist.

C. E. K. MEES, Director, Research Laboratories, Eastman Kodak Company.

CARL H. MILAM, Secretary, American Library Association.

ROBERT A. MILLIKAN, Chairman, Executive Council, California Institute of Technology.

ROBERT OLESEN, Assistant Surgeon General, U.S. Public Health Service.

THOMAS PARRAN, Surgeon General, U S. Public Health Service.

H. G. PATRICK, COMMANDER, U.S. Navy, Acting Superintendent, U.S. Naval Observatory.

JAMES ROBERTSON, Director, Nautical Almanac Office, U.S. Naval Observatory.

JAMES T. SHOTWELL, Chairman, The American National Committee on Intellectual Cooperation of the League of Nations.

ARTHUR SNOW, Assistant Director, Nautical Almanac Office, U.S. Naval Observatory.

MATTHEW STERLING, Director, Bureau of Ethnology, Smithsonian Institution.

GEORGE C. VAILLANT, Associate Curator of Mexican Archaeology, American Museum of Natural History.

C. G. WEBER, Paper Technologist, U.S. Bureau of Standards.

CLARK WISSLER, Dean of the Scientific Staff, American Museum of Natural History.

[51]

THIS BOOK and the Time Capsule which it describes have been prepared by the Westinghouse Electric & Manufacturing Company, as a contribution to the people of a future age. The book has been produced by G. Leonard Gold of the Prestige Book Company; printed by Howard Coggeshall at his Press in Utica, New York, on types* designed & arranged by Frederic W. Goudy at the Village Press in Marlborough, New York. The frontispiece was produced by Charles Furth at the Photogravure & Color Company, and the binding was planned and produced by Randall W. Bergmann of the Russell-Rutter Company, New York, in September, 1938. The paper is Permanent Ivory Wove, manufactured under the direction of Fred W. Main, especially for this book, by the Hurlbut Paper Company, South Lee, Massachusetts.

*The Vocabulary of High-frequency English, Monotype set, is in Gill sans-serif.

INDEX

Note: The follow index entries are based on the pagination of the current volume, and *not* the page numbers shown in brackets at the bottom of the facsimile pages.

I.

ABOUT THE AUTHORS

G. EDWARD PENDRAY wrote the main text of *The Book of Record*. As Assistant to the President of the Westinghouse Electric and Manufacturing Company, he directed the entire Time Capsule project.

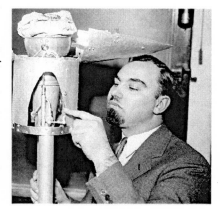

George Edward Pendray was born in Nebraska in 1901, and grew up in Wyoming. He graduated from the University of Wyoming in 1924 and received a Master's degree from Columbia University in 1925. He worked at the New York *Herald Tribune*, and was the science editor of *Literary Digest* from 1932 through 1936. In 1936 he joined Westinghouse Electric and Manufacturing Company as Assistant to the President. Pendray left Westinghouse in 1945 and started his own public relations firm, Pendray and Company.

He helped found the American Rocket Society (ARS) in 1930, a precursor to the present-day American Institute of Aeronautics and Astronautics (AIAA). The AIAA sponsors the annual Pendray Aerospace Literature Award in recognition of his achievements. In 1948, Pendray helped develop the Guggenheim Jet Propulsion Center at the California Institute of Technology, precursor to the present-day Jet Propulsion Laboratory. G. Edward Pendray died on September 5, 1987.

JOHN PEABODY HARRINGTON wrote "The Key to the English Language" section of *The Book of Record*. He was born in 1884 and raised in Santa Barbara, California. Even in his childhood, he evidenced strong interest in the local Indian tribes, and in languages. After graduation from Stanford University, he studied in Berlin and Leipzig, Germany. In 1906, he traveled back to the United States and devoted himself to the study of American Indian languages. In 1915 he was appointed as a Research Ethnologist by the Bureau of American Ethnology. For much of the next four decades, he worked to document and record Indian

language and culture, amassing treasure troves of information. After his death in 1961, curators at the Smithsonian Institution discovered that Harrington had deliberately hidden vast amounts of this material in garages, warehouses, and other such places all along the West Coast. Once collected and organized, it was found to include written records of over 125 languages, sound recordings made over many years, and thousands of photographs. Material he collected is still being studied today.

FREDERIC W. GOUDY (1865-1947) designed the special typeface used in *The Book of Record*. He was one of the leading type designers in the United States, and indeed the world. In tribute to him, the present volume is set in digital versions of Goudy Old Style and Goudy Hand-Tooled Small Capitals.

THOMAS B. ALLEN is the author or co-author of numerous books about military history and espionage. His children's books for National Geographic—*Remember Pearl Harbor, Remember Valley Forge, George Washington, Spymaster,* and *Harriet Tubman, Secret Agent,* have received outstanding reviews and won multiple awards. He lives in Bethesda, Maryland with his wife Scottie.

Visit him on the web at www.tballen.com

ROGER MACBRIDE ALLEN is the award-winning author of over twenty science fiction novels, three of them *New York Times* bestsellers. He has also published two technical manuals, and a modest number of short stories. He is Thomas B. Allen's son, and his co-author of the book *Mr. Lincoln's High-Tech War,* published by National Geographic. His wife, Eleanore Fox, is a Foreign Service Officer. They have two young sons, Matthew and James. Home base is Takoma Park, Maryland. However, Eleanore's State Department duties took the family to Mexico City for a two-to-three year posting starting in August 2010.

Visit Roger's website at www.rogermacbrideallen.com.

Roger MacBride Allen (left) and Thomas B. Allen (right) at the burial site of the two Westinghouse Time Capsules.

A Fall 2010 title from FoxAcre Press:
THE TIME CAPSULE SOURCE BOOK

IN PREPARATION for the 1939-1940 New York World's Fair, Westinghouse buried the world's first Time Capsule. Just over a quarter-century later, Time Capsule II was laid to rest 10 feet north of its older twin at the 1964-1965 Fair, to await the year 6939 A.D.

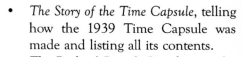

THE TIME CAPSULE SOURCE BOOK reproduces the key documents related to the Time Capsules, and provides fascinating insights into time periods that are not so far back in the past, but already seem a world away from the present. Here for the first time in one volume are the primary source documents concerning both Time Capsules:

- *The Story of the Time Capsule*, telling how the 1939 Time Capsule was made and listing all its contents.
- *The Book of Record*: Simply put, the instruction manual on how to find the Capsules—a letter, addressed to our ancestors, 5,000 years from now.
- A list of U.S. and overseas recipients of *The Book of Record*.
- *The Report of the Westinghouse Time Capsule II Selections Committee*, with a full and detailed list of all the contents of the 1965 Time Capsule.
- The Groundbreaking Brochure for the 1964-1965 Westinghouse Exhibit, showing exactly how the Capsules were buried.
- Film stills and magazine advertising showing the adventures of the Middletons at the 1939 World's Fair
- Introductions and commentary explaining all the documents.

The Time Capsule Source Book documents a fascinating tale of the dreamers and thinkers of the past—and the efforts they made to send two messengers far into the future.

FoxAcre.com
TimeCapsuleBook.com